Ouch,

THERE'S A PEBBLE IN MY SHOE

by Cheryl P. Gainey

DORRANCE
PUBLISHING CO
EST. 1920
PITTSBURGH, PENNSYLVANIA 15238

Dorrance Publishing Co
585 Alpha Drive
Pittsburgh, PA 15238
Visit our website at *www.dorrancebookstore.com*

ISBN: 978-1-6366-1309-3
eISBN: 978-1-6366-1893-7

Dedication

This collection of poems is dedicated to Jennifer, Terrence, and Terrell, and all who gave me an enormous amount of encouragement and support. Thank each and every one of you so much for seeing what was inside of me, when I didn't see it in myself. I could not have taken such a giant leap of faith, without any of you. I thank my mother, Arlene for her support as well. Love you all.

Table of Contents

The Canvas

A blank canvas, no ink, has touched the surface. But one day something happened. That ink fell on the canvas. The ink begun to look like a dot, as small as a period, used in a sentence.

Then as time went on, the ink spot, became a little bigger, and became a family of many dots, connecting themselves together. The dots started to represent different colors and shapes; you begin to wonder what's happening to this canvas. What does it mean?

The dots on the canvas start to move in many different directions. Where are they going? The dot began to say, "Don't leave me," and you start feeling all alone. You remember the dots were meant to spend time together, but now, you are the only dot left on the canvas. Just like when you first came on the scene. You look to the right, and you look to the left. Were you meant to be on this canvas alone? Where did the other dots go? What do you do? Who and what tried to erase the dots from the canvas?

The dot is very curious, it feels abandoned. It feels afraid to branch out, so the dot gets in the only position that it knows how. The dot moves to the brush, so that it can be used to fill the entire canvas. Because the dot and the canvas now know that they were meant to be together until the end. It's finish.

Can't you see the beautiful piece of art on that canvas? You were fearfully and wonderfully made. (Psalm 139:14)

Criticized but Chosen

You are on your knees
Praying to God

In the privacy of your room,
The door opens, and
someone comes in.

You know you're chosen
but all you hear is the criticism
that cuts down deep within
You freeze in your place
and stop praying

Criticized or chosen?
you ask yourself

Criticism will come,
but you have to let it go
because you have been chosen
before you experienced criticism,
so you begin to pray again!

You no longer need to stand
in criticism's shoes, because
they don't fit anymore.
Yet criticized, but chosen.

Chosen are the shoes that were
meant to fit, they are not too
tight, nor are they too big.
Chosen was custom made
just for you by the Creator.

Chosen is fearfully and wonderfully
made, in the image that was purposed
just for you.

So goodbye criticism,
I can no longer wear you,
like I wore a heavy winter coat.
Because chosen is a much better fit,
so now I choose chosen over criticism.

Dare to Dream

It's raining outside, and the birds are chirping in the tree.
People are walking to and fro, some with umbrellas and some not.
Few cars are passing, but buses are not.

As those things pass, in my mind, I dare to dream. Someone
made those umbrellas that people are holding. Someone made
those cars that people are driving. Someone owns
those stores that I went in and/or passed by.

So, why can't I dare to dream? I want to be free, like the birds
in the tree. As the birds soar high up in the sky, why can't I?
Every car, every truck, every bicycle, every motorcycle, that
passes by, I dare to dream.

Every book, newspaper that I read, I dare to dream.
Every television program that I watch, I dare to dream.

Dare to dream.

What do you see, when you dare to dream?

Fear Is Forward Faith

With closed eyes, you feel yourself moving so fast over the road nothing like a highway, but on top of the mountain of tall trees. You try to put on the brakes to stop what feels like a speed chase, but you keep going full speed ahead, hoping this ride would end right then and there.

However, you're still up on that highway of mountain of tall trees. You feel that this is the longest ride of your life and you fear going any further. You regretfully look down from the mountaintop, you tightly close your eyes from fear of what you continue to see and feel. Inwardly you cry, please stop, I can't stand to look anymore, but you still see the height of the mountain of trees and feel the intensity of the speed.

Then you start to see that you're on familiar ground, where you begin to recognize that you're back in civilization, where you see people, cars, and a train station. You feel a sigh of relief. Then the voice from the driver speaks these words: Have faith, no matter what you see, how fast life may be moving, you must have faith.

If you have the faith, the size of a mustard seed, it will outgrow the False Evidence Appearing Real. (F.E.A.R.).

Greater Things

Have you ever wondered,
what was happening,
when someone unknown to you,
encouraged you with a
pen and a piece of paper?

That kind of encouragement came to me,
when I saw this young lady sitting on a bus,
in front of me, with a pen and pad in her hand.

Just like the one you may have in your pocketbook,
but you have not been using.

You saw the pen in the person's hand
contemplating what they were writing
on that pad, then such a strong feeling
comes over you, that you should be writing.

You tell that person, "thank you,"
for the encouragement, still not knowing
what she was writing, you just see
words, but you can't make it out.
It could have been a grocery list,
for all you know, but that does not
matter. All you see are words on the paper.

The two of you are now sitting on the bus,
writing on your pads. Now, you feel that this
is what you should be doing.
And you start saying to yourself,
"I can do all things, through Christ,
who strengthens me." (Philippians 4:13)

It somehow feels much bigger than you,
and you feel you can't accomplish
what you have set your mind to.

You remember, not only did this young lady
encourage you, to write, but you start to
hear a poetic writer's voice,
strongly and constantly encouraging you.

The writer in you is now dying to come forth,
like rivers of flowing water.

Tell yourself that "You Can" and "You Will"
see it come to pass; you are now on the road
to greater things!

I Feel the Spirit All Over Me

As I sit and read my daily bible reading: Ephesians 1:15-23 (Thanksgiving and Prayer), thank you, Lord, for giving me your strength and your spirit and keeping me in your prayers. Thank you for your wisdom – teach me to use it when necessary. I would especially thank you for the last verse of Ephesians (which is his body, the fullness of him who fills everything in every way). There is no way not to understand this last verse because it is true in the full spectrum of the verse. Again, as I look back over my life, you have filled me with your song, your word, and last but not least – your spirit. Thank you for not forsaking me. "I feel the spirit all over me."

The Journey

How is one's journey described?
The journey is like taking a long
long walk. It has a starting and an
ending point.

But what's more important, is what
you do between the two points. You
are born, but your journey did not
start there, it begun before you were
born, if you can believe that.

Where are you on the journey? Have
you figured out what the word journey even
means in your life? You may have
made many detours and turns, but
has those detours prevented you from
moving forward? Don't stop,
don't stay stuck, keep on moving forward,
because more water has to be
poured into you, so the seed inside of you can grow.

The journey, if you could imagine,
is like running water, it keeps flowing
until you turn the faucet off. So, what
is flowing in your vision, that you
can't rest until it happens?
The Journey - "For I know the thoughts that I think toward you says the
Lord, thoughts of peace and not evil, to give you a future and a hope".
(Jeremiah 29:11 - NKJV)

The journey, oh the journey is sweet,
even though moments are as dark as
a black pigeon sitting on your windowsill
as though it is dead, and refuses to move,
but once you have a vision, you will be
pushed until something happens. What is it
that you see, not with your natural eye, but
your spiritual eye?

Now that you see it, moving forward, hand
in hand with the journey, you must not doubt.
Because the journey has one thing in mind,
and that's to get you where you need to be.
Looking Straight Ahead.

Looking Straight Ahead

Have you ever felt like
you wanted to cry?
It's okay, go ahead and cry
But why cry? You ask yourself,
You don't know,
why you want to cry.

You tell yourself,
everything is well,
as expected, but
why can't it be better

You feel like crying,
but it hurts too much to cry

Little do you know
it's a cry of joy
because deep down
inside, you feel like
something big and
better is about to happen

Go on and cry
it will open
your peripheral vision.
Looking Straight Ahead

Look Up

Walking outside on a beautiful day
The trees were swaying back and forth
The air was crisp and clear
All of a sudden, you look up
To your surprise, the sun speaks
volumes, like never before

It beams down like a
mother's hand gently
touching your face.

You never felt the sun
like that before.
It leaves your mouth
open in wonder and in awe.
and asking the question,
Were you taking nature for granted?

You wonder, what was I thinking,
That - that gentle touch could be from the sun
caused me to see the sun in a
different light.

You start to give thanks to GOD
for that gentle touch.

It begins to saturate your thoughts
with gratefulness and acknowledges
the presence of God.
He is everywhere at all times.

Look up and feel God's gentleness
Look up and feel
Look up and feel God's loving care
Just look up!

Love Me

As I sat in the auditorium of a local high school, honoring Martin Luther King, Jr., at "The Central Brooklyn Martin Luther King, Jr. Commission." I looked at a picture that was displayed on the stage and asked myself, "what can I do to be like Martin Luther King, Jr."? - a small still voice spoke to me, by saying, "Love Me". So, I know now, that not just because Martin Luther King, Jr. loved GOD, I MUST Love GOD for myself, because HE first loved me.

Never Alone

I searched and searched in my bag
for my cell phone, I could not find it.
Earlier I went to a women's conference at church,
So I thought that I left it on the table.
I could not call anyone to have them call my phone,
nor was anyone else in the house with me,
So I could use their cell phone, to find my phone.
It felt like I was all alone, but no, I was not.
I came to my senses and realized
that in the quietness of the night, God is there.
I also realized whenever I am alone,
that is the time God is waiting for me
to have a little talk with Jesus,
so I need to wait for God to speak to me.

God may not speak right away, but He does speak,
While waiting for the train
I realized that I just have to listen. Thank you, LORD!

Amazing Grace
How sweet the sound
That saved a wretch like me

I once was lost
But now I'm found
Was blind, but now I see.

(and)

When trouble rise
I'll hasten to His Throne.

The Other Side of the Mountain

On the local bus,
that stops at every,
single stop

Life can sometimes move as
slow as that
local bus,
When you're
trying to get
somewhere

Things are going
slow, keep moving
forward, there is
something waiting
for you on the
other side of
the mountain.

Something bigger
and greater that
you could not have
imagined nor see,
is on the other side
of the mountain.

Not only is it bigger
and greater, it's
better. But continue
to move forward,
not looking back.

No matter how fast
or slow, you can make it
to the other side of
the mountain.

Moving to the other
side of the mountain,
there's something
waiting for you, on the other
side of the mountain.

Over the Bridge

The bridge can get you
across to one borough
to another –

The bridge has a walking
and a driving experience

Driving in a car is cool
But walking has a different
experience all together

You're walking across
and you reached the other
side pretty fast, you
realized that you made
it to your destination
already.

How did you get across so
quickly, you didn't feel your feet,
hitting the pavement –
You were carried across!

You stood still for a moment,
you truly realized that
you were carried across

You think you were only
carried across the bridge,
but no, you were carried
throughout your whole
life – through the good
and the bad.

You are being carried right
now – over troubled waters
through the fire and through
the flood.

Who carried you over that
bridge?

Passionate Partner

The clock goes tick tock,
the passion is also moving
right along with the clock.

Passion will never, ever stop
like the clock, once passion
comes along, it just gets
stronger and stronger.

When passion is felt,
it may make you become
afraid, because passion
is so much bigger than
you are.

Passion knocks and keeps
on knocking. Passion will
never leave you along.
Passion may even cause you
to cry tears of joy like never
before.

Passion becomes your
passionate partner.
Passion walks with you
wherever you go.
Passion talks to you when
nobody else will
Passion will give you words
that you never thought
you could say.
Passion can make you
want to be whatever
your heart desires.

Get to know the passionate partner.

Purpose or Pain

Purpose moves forward
In and out of season.

Purpose always moves
from one place
to another.

Purpose may be in pain,
but it does not stand
nor sits still

Pain, yes it hurts,
but if there is purpose
in you, purpose would
make you run when
nobody's chasing you.

Pain is locked in the moment,
But when purpose shows up,
if it has to take pain with it,
Purpose will press its way
through and pain would
have to go.

Purpose takes over pain
Purpose is more powerful than pain
Purpose is defined by destiny
But pain is defined by the past.
Which one defines you?
Purpose or pain?

Shattered Dreams

Can we talk for a moment?

As I think about our relationship, something comes to mind.

I always wanted to know, did you ever have any dreams that you have not achieved, dreams that you put on the back burner? What were they? Did you want to be a doctor, nurse, or a lawyer? Or even write a book?

Did someone shatter your dreams that they never came to fruition? Did you forget to dream? Or did you ever notice it in a vision? Did you ever feel like you wanted more? Did your dream(s) make you afraid, because you didn't understand what was happening to you?

Can we talk about your shattered dreams?

Song of Praise

Dear Lord,

You are so good to me even when I don't deserve it. As I was coming up the stairs at a familiar train station, you put the song, "Stomp" in my spirit. Thank you for your gift of song. It is the best thing for my soul, besides the WORD of God. I ask you to help me to remember and keep bringing those precious songs out of my spirit, because I need to be ministered by them – Thank you, thank you, Lord, for giving me your song of praise.

Stand Up, You Giant

Stand up, there is a giant in you.
You say, "You can't."
How do you know until you try?

Pick up that pen or pencil
and write that poem, play,
movie, or book.

Let it flow, and when you do,
that giant inside of you
will make room for you.

Just imagine yourself
doing something that
you didn't think you could do.

It's never too late,
but you have to believe
that there is a giant
inside of you,
waiting to come out.

Don't be afraid, the giant
will not let you down
nor hurt you.

What is your giant?
Do you see it?
If not, look a little closer,
it will eventually show,
itself to you.

Now stand up and look
for it, it's right there,
inside of you!.

The Sun Set and My Cheek

One sunny, hot day
Walking down the street,
with thoughts running,
through my mind.

Not realizing it,
I kept walking
Then I noticed the sun

As my head lifted
I felt a gentle touch
across my cheek

When I realized what happened,
my eyes were opened.
Things began to look
differently and I
began to see a lot clearer,
as never before.

To be gently kissed by the sun,
felt amazing, as though it,
literally came down and
touched my face

Wow, did that really
just happen?
It was a touch that was
never ever felt before

Was the sun used to
get my attention?
I don't know, but I
would not forget how
God lovingly touched me
through the sun.

The sun set on my cheek,
but only for a few seconds,
that it felt so sleek,
out of maybe feelings
so bleak, the sun set
on my cheek!

Thinkable Thoughts

Have you ever thought about the thoughts
that you think?

The thoughts that travel through
your brain waves, moves quite
frequently through the day.
Within a twenty-four hour
time span, you would be
surprised as to how many thoughts
you've had before you
retire for the night.

Some of those thoughts are good
but can you be honest with
yourself, some can be pretty bad.

Some of those thoughts can
cause you to do good and not so good.
Do you live life going from
doing good to doing bad
and doing bad to doing good.

Do you let every thought control
your actions? If so, what would
your life look like? Pretty good or pretty bad?

So, challenge yourself to think of whatever is true, whatever is noble,
whatever is right, whatever is pure,
whatever is lovely, whatever is admirable—
if anything is excellent or praiseworthy—
think about such things. And the God of peace
will be with you.

The thoughts that have been invading
your thought pattern would
have to change

Welcome Eyes

I looked in your eyes and
I saw what I never
wanted to look at before

When I looked in your eyes
Your soul shined so radiant
and bright in my eyes that
Confident finally took a front seat

Through your eyes, I could
feel your strength because
Through your eyes, strong was
the strength, it almost made
me run; but the pull was so
STRONG, it stopped me in
my tracks, that I couldn't run,
and I didn't want to either
I was determined to see more
when I looked in your eyes

As I looked in your eyes, I felt secure
So, stay with me a while, and
stop by more, in your eyes
is where I want to be.

In your eyes, I know that I will
make it through because your
eyes tell me to be strong and
courageous, that you will never
leave me, nor forsake me.
Your Welcome Eyes tell me so.